Aural Time!

Practice Tests for ABRSM and Other Exams

Grade 3

DAVID TURNBULL

CONTENTS

Bosworth

INTRODUCTION

Aural training has always been of the greatest importance to teachers and their pupils. In recent years, however, the emphasis has changed from depending on memory skills to the development of a wider general sense of awareness. The Associated Board of the Royal Schools of Music has given impetus to change by designing new tests for Grade 1 to 5 from January 1993.

Teachers may like to use this booklet to supplement the aural training material they devise for themselves. Like most musical skills, aural awareness needs regular training and practice, and aural work should be part of every lesson.

Not all good instrumental teachers are necessarily fluent pianists. Most of the tests in this booklet therefore have simple pianoforte accompaniments. **If necessary, even these accompaniments can be omitted, and the tests given as melodic lines only.** Much use is made of songs, and it is hoped that the tests will stimulate further interest in this great area of musical achievement.

Teachers may like to use some of the tests in Section A as additional Section D material by using varied dynamics, tempo markings etc.

David Turnbull

September 1992

Test A. Tapping Test.   GRADE 3

Tap the pulse of the piece of music, which will be in 2 (including 6/8), or 3 time (including 9/8), or 4 time. Join in with your tapping as soon as you can, stressing where the strong beats fall. Be prepared to say what time the piece is in.

International Copyright Secured

B. & Co. Ltd., 22288

2

Andante

Scottish trad.: *Will Ye No Come Back Again?*

5

Moderato

Breton trad.: *Pieds en l'air*

6

Allegro non troppo

French trad.: *La Mère Michel*

7

Moderato

Stephen Foster: *Massa's in de Cold, Cold Ground*

8

Test B. Echoes.

Sing, as echoes, three short phrases played to you. The echoes should follow each played phrase in strict time, without an intervening pause. The key-chord and the tonic will first be sounded and the pulse indicated.

Test C. Recognising Changes.

Recognise and explain a rhythmic or melodic change to a four-bar phrase in a major or minor key played over twice. The key-chord and tonic will first be sounded.

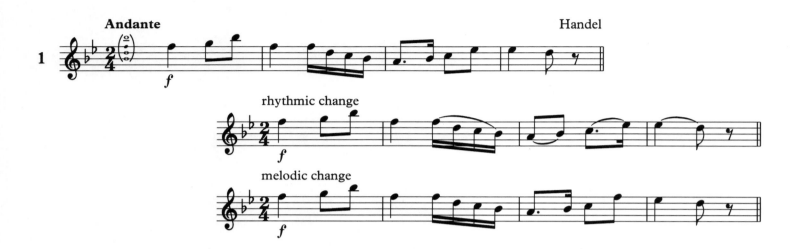

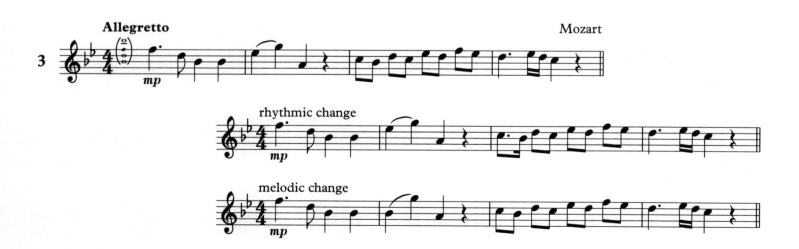

12

Test D. Recognising Features.

Identify certain features of a piece played over to you. The features will be confined to contrasted dynamics (*p*/*f*), gradation of tone (*crescendo*/*diminuendo*), articulation (*staccato*/*legato*) and recognition of tempo changes (*rallentando*/*accelerando* etc.) and recognition of major and minor modes. Use Italian terms in your answers where appropriate. The piece, or any section of it, can be repeated if neccessary.

Haydn: "*Surprise*" *Symphony*

Questions:
    a. Is the piece in a major or minor key?
    b. Is the music mostly *staccato* or *legato*?
    c. Which was the loudest part?
    d. Was it played at a steady tempo?

Schumann (adapted)

Questions:
    a. Is the piece in a major or minor key?
    b. Did the music get gradually louder or softer? If so, where?
    c. Was it mainly *legato, staccato,* or a mixture of both?
    d. Was it played at a steady tempo? If not, where did the tempo change?

Allegro non troppo

Schumann (adapted)

Questions:
  a. Is the piece in a major or minor key?
  b. Did the music get gradually louder or softer? If so, where?
  c. Was it mainly *legato, staccato,* or a mixture of both?
  d. Was it played at a steady tempo? If not, where did the tempo change?

Allegretto

Purcell (adapted)

Questions:
  a. Describe the dynamics of the music.
  b. Does it begin *staccato* or *legato*?
  c. Does it end *staccato* or *legato*?
  d. Are there any alterations to tempo? If so where?
  e. Is it in a major or a minor key?

B. & Co. Ltd., 22288

Moderato

Telemann (adapted)

Questions:
- a. Is the piece in a major or minor key?
- b. Describe the dynamics of the music.
- c. Was it mainly *legato*, or *staccato*, or a mixture of both?
- d. Was it played at a steady tempo? If not, where did the tempo change?

Moderato

Tchaikovsky (adapted)

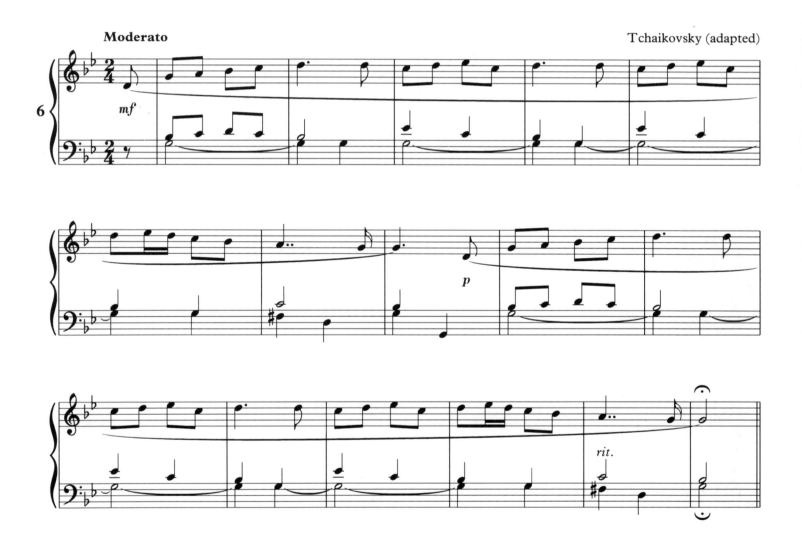

Questions:
- a. Is the piece in a major or minor key?
- b. Describe the dynamics of the music.
- c. Was it mainly *legato*, or *staccato*, or a mixture of both?
- d. Was it played at a steady tempo? If not, where and how did the tempo change?

Czerny (adapted)

Questions:
   a. Is the piece in a major or minor key?
   b. Did the music get gradually louder or softer? If so, where?
   c. Was it mainly *legato*, *staccato*, or a mixture of both?
   d. Was it played at a steady tempo? If not, where did the tempo change?

Mendelssohn

Questions:
   a. Did the music start in a major or minor key?
   b. Did it end in a major or a minor key?
   c. Did the music become gradually louder or softer? If so, where?
   d. Was it played at a steady tempo? If not, where and how did the tempo change?

B. & Co. Ltd., 22288

Questions:

    a. Did the tempo of the music alter? If so, how?

    b. Did the music begin *legato* or *staccato*?

    c. Was it in a major key or a minor key?

    d. Describe the dynamics.

(If playing the melodic line without accompaniment, play notes in brackets.)

Questions:

    a. Did the music start in a major key or a minor key?

    b. Did it end in a major key or a minor key?

    c. Was there any alteration in the tempo?

    d. Describe the dynamics of the music.

Printed in England by
Caligraving Limited Thetford Norfolk

B. & Co. Ltd., 22288

1/09(168230)